28 Steps to Save Your Job - and everyone else's!

Turning Intuition into Evidence

A practical programme for Learning and Development Professionals

Maria Paviour

28 Steps has been designed to:

- Drive emotional engagement through learning
- Improve business performance
- Prove your worth to your senior team
- Demonstrate the value of your entire Learning and Development department

28 Steps to Save Your Job - and Everyone Else's!

Third Edition

ISBN: 0-9543654-4-8

http://www.mariapaviour.com
http://www.isynergizelife.com

Acknowledgements and thanks:
Thanks chiefly to Polly Pomfrey for her fabulous work on pulling this book into shape for me, editing, designing and adding so much of her own wit and wisdom to it.

Thanks to Cole Paviour for his wonderful illustrations.

Preface

As an Occupational Psychologist, Educator, Author and Business Manager my passion for employee engagement, psychological well-being and workplace happiness has extended over 25 years. So I have spent my career having fun! Hooray!

There are two kinds of engagement at work in business today: Transactional Engagement in which people love the job or career, but are not that fussed about the organisation; and Emotional Engagement in which they love the organisation for which they work and may not be so fussed about what they do in it.

I specialise in Emotional Engagement.

Transactional Engagement may look positive, but it creates a lot of stress and staff turnover may be higher than you would like. Emotionally Engaged people invest energy, rather than feeling stress; they are more likely to have better mental health and less likely to have sickness absence.

It must be a given that all businesses are only as successful as their people make them. And for those who doubt this then a look at the evidence proves that where engagement is high, performance is top quartile in virtually every respect.

So where does one start in achieving high levels of emotional engagement and reaping the benefits of double the profit and business growth?

The number one trust relationship in organisations is between employees and their First Line Managers. So ensuring Managers have adequate skills is your single most important task. If you are going to influence your organisation to succeed then you need to begin by ensuring that none of your managers fly under the radar.

And the second key ingredient to emotional engagement is a sense of self-efficacy in all your people; in other words that they believe in themselves.

If you can make a difference in these two areas you will begin a groundswell of change. And when you do, don't forget to ensure you get your fair share of credit for it!

All the best,

Maria

Introduction

I first came up with the idea of *'28 Steps to Save Your Job - and Everyone Else's!'* when I noticed the squeeze that certain organisations were putting on their Learning and Development (L&D) departments.

After being in the people development business for twenty years I felt frustrated that, even after all this time, the true value of L&D was being missed by certain board directors of certain rather large organisations.

You already have the answer

For years, those of us in L&D have known, have felt in our water, that the solution to many of the difficulties in business could be solved by developing people; by providing them with opportunities to learn new ways of acting and being; and by enabling managers to develop the skills they need to support, nurture and facilitate excellence in their teams.

We have known this intuitively, but we have struggled when the big pound note signs have been thrown down on the table. How could we argue with a cost benefit analysis, or a financially driven strategic plan?

Well, you can.

Your intuition can now become an evidence base for success.

One of the ironies of the current economy is the way in which some L&D people have either lost, or been unable to develop, really healthy levels of self confidence in their own value to the business. We often see ourselves as slightly less important and relevant as Finance or Marketing or Production. When we sit at the board table, often only invited there occasionally rather than as a matter of course, we feel that we may be there for some "on the ground" anecdotes, rather than because we have a strong basis in fact upon which the entire future of the business can be determined.

Challenging the Guru

My vision for *'28 Steps to Save Your Job – and Everyone Else's'* is to support Learning and Development professionals in seeing the huge value that they have in the business. I don't care what anyone says, find me a business that succeeds without great people and I'll retire tomorrow! Every business relies on its people. So before there is some big hatchet campaign to save money and cull jobs, let's do our utmost to make every moment count in developing the skills in our people, and most importantly, all you Learning and Development Professionals recognise the tremendous value that you bring to the business; the often unseen and unappreciated value. Get into your self-belief and realise that unless you are in post and doing what you do best you cannot save everyone else!

Some parts of this programme may push you and challenge you. Well, start thinking of yourself as the business performance Guru and you will know that you can rise to that challenge.

There is always a risk in business. For you, the risk is to be seen, and recognised. And about time too, in my view.

How to use this book

Each Step is a key stage for you to work through.

- Put your energy into following the steps one at a time, consecutively.
- If you have already completed some of the stages, you can simply accelerate through that section.
- Do complete all the steps! Take them one at a time, and be sure to go through each one.
- Find the quickest and easiest way to get the maximum results – try not to overthink.
- Don't go for perfection! Get something started, and then improve it. Don't persist in trying to improve something you don't yet have.
- Keep going. If you get half way and don't complete it you will achieve nothing! Completion is vital. Drop me an email (hello@mariapaviour.com) if you need some support or you're not sure about something.

Remember, thinking BIG has never prevented anyone from being successful - but thinking small has!

Chapter 1: Why you MUST save your job – why YOU are essential in the success of the business

Introducing Steps 1-4

Bear with me, it may seem that I'm going to state the obvious during this introduction... There is a good reason though!

In recent years there has been a revolution in self-awareness. The market for self-help books and self-help programmes has exploded. The same also needs to happen in the economy: we all need to raise our business-awareness.

Let me explain. Before I can begin to work with any of my clients I must have a clear handle on the business. So the first thing I do is research: who, what, where, how long, history

Then I need to find out some of the less obvious information: what they want to achieve; aspirations; values; culture; view on the world and their market

Once I have a clear picture in my own mind, I can begin to think about working with them.

What is interesting is that not all the people I work with really know or understand their own business's vision. And, many have re-invented it to suit their own department!

I am amazed at how often a department will choose to take its own approach to these questions. And often this heralds the problems that exist within the business; failure to communicate across departments, individual differences and, most damaging of all, the inherent failure to make decisions.

No matter how large the business, there must be a common set of values and aspirations, and it is vital that you not only know what these are, but are fully prepared to be engaged with them.

It may seem obvious that you must align your plans with the business objectives

But, in my experience, I rarely see this carried out fully and completely.

It is quite commonplace for L&D professionals, for example, to tell me that they are carrying out a Needs Analysis of their entire staff (more on that later), but I hardly ever hear them tell me that they have first carried out a Needs Analysis on what the **business** wants or needs.

Frequently this is based upon anecdotal evidence from senior managers who have complained about poor performance in an individual (which may become a reason for carrying out an entire programme of learning) or that it is a failure of senior managers to effectively adapt to different working styles. It is rarely a full analysis of vision, mission, a business scorecard or any other method for identifying where the business is doing well or falling behind expectation or aspiration.

When intuition is not enough

You cannot expect to gain full support and engagement in your idea if you have not gained the essential "buy in" from senior management or business owners or stakeholders. And on the other hand, you cannot be expected to be successful if you are basing your entire programme on a handful of neither scored nor weighted anecdotal evidence. You may intuitively know something is needed, but without actual evidence…

I am not, at this point, talking about discussions that occur at the board table where you may well be able to put forward an excellent example of management skills development. What I do refer to are specific aspects of the vision to which your plan will dovetail so seamlessly and naturally, that it will be obvious that the business cannot continue without it. That it is essential for success.

If your plan cannot do that then you have no business implementing it.

Working in the rarefied world of Learning and Development can cause you to lose touch with the basic business facts while you enjoy basking in the creativity of your role.

I am all in favour of creativity in business, and this is not in any way intended to undervalue that. On the contrary, this programme is intended to help you to use your creativity in such a way that it is instrumental in creating a solid and fundamentally profitable business.

In that way, you can ensure you save your own job, and help all the company's employees to save their own too.

And it is vital that you DO save your job; as in this economic environment where businesses are feeling the pinch, it is the worst of all decisions to cut back on those elements that will make you more profitable, more effective and ultimately sustainable.

Learning and Development is the future of successful businesses, and so now is the time to ensure that you prove the value of what you bring to your business.

STEP 1: Why is being a nosy parker essential to success?

- ### The Four KEY factors in knowing your business

If you are to save your job, you need to start by being nosy. Yes, nosy! There are four key factors in knowing your business, and you need to be nosy enough to uncover each and every one of them.

The Four KEY factors in knowing your business: mission; vision; values; strategy

A **Mission** statement tells you the fundamental purpose of the organization. It defines the customer and the critical processes. It informs you of the desired level of performance.

A **Vision** statement outlines what the organization wants to be, or how it wants the world in which it operates to be. It concentrates on the future. It is a source of inspiration. It provides clear decision-making criteria.

- It is vital that you have a clear idea of the Vision in your head as this will inspire you.
- You must have the Mission in mind as this will guide your planning

The other elements that you must have well formulated in your plan are:

Values: Beliefs that are shared among the stakeholders of an organization. Values drive an organization's culture and priorities and provide a framework in which decisions are made. For example, "Learning is fun and the basis of our daily life" This sets the scene for our people to appreciate that learning is core to their working day, that it is expected and that we find it enjoyable.

Strategy: Strategy narrowly defined, means "the art of the general" (from Greek stratigos). Your strategy is a combination of the goal you wish to achieve and the method by which you intent to achieve it.

The business values must be at the heart of any plans that you devise. The strategy will be the plan. At this stage, we will leave strategy until later in the programme. Right now we need to be clear about the aims and vision.

STEP 1 ACTION PLAN: Get nosy: research and understand the business vision and mission

Pinpoint, identify, uncover or create your business purpose.

STEP 2: Mix Your Ps and Qs – Question, Plan, Question

- **Why plan? Why question?**
- **Why asking about biscuits may not work**
- **Questions that have real value**

Why plan? Why question?

In case you hadn't guessed, this is all about planning your questionnaire…

How do you determine your business's vision (inspiration) and mission (purpose)?

The obvious method - which you probably completed for Step 1 - is to read the vision statement, mission statement and any strategic plans that have been disseminated.

Going further, to really get value and truth you could speak to the senior people in the business, and ask them what they would most like the business to achieve; what they believe are the key values; what clients or customers they wish to develop; how they like to work.

Carry out a survey on your senior team or business stakeholders. www.surveymonkey.com is a good free (initially) tool to use for this.

What should I ask? What's their favourite biscuit?

Hmm. Well you could… but it would be more valuable to think about what the key questions are that you need answers to.

These questions are vital, as they should always be identifying where there is a problem - and the solution to that problem is where you and your creative mind can come into play! But don't worry, if you are not having a very creative moment, I will guide you on the areas upon which you need to focus, and I will help you in how to solve any of those problems (later on in this programme) .

Questions you need to ask	Examples
What are your core services?	Air travel; Investment services; Television and radio programmes.
What are your core values?	Innovation; Integrity; Environmental care.
Over what period do you want to make the vision last?	
What do you want the business to look like at the end of that period?	Examples: The most profitable in the industry; Increase profits by 150%; Increase sales by 300%.
What will make your business successful over this period?	Increased marketing activity; Improved product quality; Improved customer service; improved effectiveness.
Where is your market?	Local; Regional; International.
What is your passion?	

Here are some sample questions which have been used by another company:

Vision/Mission Questions

- If our business could be what we want in ten years, what would it be?
- What new activities will our business be pursuing? What business will we be in?
- Who will be the customers of our business?
- What customer needs will our business satisfy?
- What will be the new roles and responsibilities of employees and stakeholders involved in the business?

- What will we be especially good at? What will make our business unique?
- What do we envision for our staff?

STEP 2 ACTION PLAN: Get mixing – plan your questionnaire

Identify key priorities by asking the right questions of the right people.

STEP 3: How will swotting pests turn intuition into evidence?

- **How the SWOT analysis is a FUNDAMENTAL framework**
- **PEST – the key external issues you MUST face head on**

This isn't just about fly bashing – a karmically unsound practice at best!

In business, SWOT and PEST are two extremely powerful strategic analysis tools. Use them to learn about the internal and external factors that may affect what you are planning.

The SWOT analysis - One of the fundamental frameworks.

This is a simple tool, for identifying the key areas to which you need to focus your attention.

SWOT Chart:
Strengths, Weaknesses, Opportunities, Threats

	Internal: why should the customer buy?		How do you plan to counter weaknesses and threats?
How to you plan to respond/build upon strengths and opportunities?	STRENGTHS	WEAKNESSES	
	External: political, economic, social, technological		
	OPPORTUNITIES	THREATS	

In the chart you can see that I have added questions to ask yourself when you are faced with your answers - what are you going to do about weakness and threats; this may be where you plan will come strongly into operation.

I have also noted the key external issues which come under the heading of PEST analysis - they are:

Political, Economic, Social, Technological

These external PEST factors are VITALLY IMPORTANT RIGHT NOW!

They are the most likely to affect your position in your company and its future success.

Just review what has happened in the last few years, the economic downturn, the banking crisis, the problem of massive government debts. All these things are likely to affect your security and the businesses success.

You MUST face these head on, look at how they may affect your business, and then ensure that you develop your plan and present it so that you can use the power of the people, their skills and their potential to create a profitable business; and therefore a secure business.

STEP 3 ACTION PLAN: Create your analysis using SWOT and PEST

Think about your business in today's market and your role.

STEP 4: Melding the visions

- Turning the business vision into a *people development* vision
- How people make successful business, not the other way round
- How to frame vision questions

Turn the business vision into a *people development vision*

From the example questions in previous Steps, you will get a clear picture of what your business is striving for. Once you have this, clarify it in terms of what the *people* in the business can do to make it happen.

People make successful business

In the end, whether you use low, medium or high level technology, whether you have high street stores or sell on-line, whether you are a niche business or a volume business, whether you are a high fashion product like Jimmy Choo shoes or a basic and essential product like Knights Castille soap you are going to need *your people* to make a successful business of it.

Frame the vision questions, then meld with Learning and Development

So to turn all those business vision questions and answers into something you can relate to the learning and development of your business you will need to frame them in the following terms:

- What do we need to BE LIKE as people to achieve this?
- What do we need to DO as people or as managers to achieve this?
- What do we need to be AIMING FOR OR PLANNING to achieve this?
- What do we need to FOSTER IN OUR CLIENTS to achieve this?

STEP 4 ACTION PLAN: Turn the business vision into a people development vision

Put your business' Vision and Mission into people development terms.

CHAPTER 2: People and Profit: Don't be afraid of measuring success in terms of money

Introducing Steps 5, 6, and 7.

The real value of anything is usually an intrinsic feeling. We don't measure the things that really matter in terms of money, do we? For example, we don't measure our relationships, partners, or children in those terms.

In the world of Learning and Development, when faced with the idea that we have to put a price on concepts and services that are intrinsically beneficial, a lot of gnashing and wailing can occur. We worry that we might lose all the good stuff, for want of a measurable that can be related to a sum of money.

MY ADVICE:

- **Don't be afraid of measurements.**
- **Remember - you do not have to measure everything!**

The second piece of advice will help calm your mind over the first piece.

We often get into a mind-set that if we are asked to prove our effectiveness then we have to prove that EVERYTHING WE DO is effective. The fact is, that much of what we do will lead up to the end result, and it is the end result that is the true measure of effectiveness.

This does not mean that we do not have to measure *anything* as we go, but it does mean that we have to co-ordinate qualitative and quantitative measures.

Qualitative measures - these will measure quality and are therefore used to measure the level of skill an individual has attained and used.

Quantitative measures - these measure number, so may be used to measure the amount of knowledge (such as by the number of right answers in a question paper) or the amount of sales made in number or in value, the cost savings that have been made.

When you are thinking about how you can demonstrate that your People will make you a Profit you need to adopt some fluid, and creative thinking. Now, knowing my clients, this will be music to their ears, because most of them LOVE to apply their creative thinking.

On the other hand, how you focus that creativity may be making you feel like you may be about to come out in hives!

Do not fear, this is what I have spent twenty years helping my clients with. We will need to start by reviewing what we mean by Return on your Investment – which leads us nicely in to Step 5.

STEP 5: Is ROI really a big bad wolf?

- **Making People a Return on Investment**
- **ROI Analysis and Thinking**
- **ROI Thinking: using creativity to map potential**

Making people a return on investment

Most people in business these days have heard of the ROI or Return on Investment model. It has always been particularly tricky to apply with Learning and Development, and trickiness can create fear. Step 5 is all about removing the fear. Come with me as I shine the cold light of science and common sense on ROI!

ROI (Return On Investment) Analysis and Thinking

Because ROI is tricky to apply to L&D, you need to adopt two distinct methods of approaching and applying the concept: ROI Analysis and ROI thinking

- ROI Analysis (counting)

This involves making careful and duplicable measurements that prove that you have created a financial improvement through your actions.

For example, if you have carried out a training course with managers on how to deal with conflict in the workplace, you will need to show a number that demonstrates that this course has created a financial return.

This can be achieved by creating a financial value for the skills, and then reviewing the skills level of an individual before and after the event:

Example: Financial value for a skill - Doctor's Receptionist

- Communicating face to face with difficult, aggressive patients.
- Estimated time spent on this task/activity in terms of percentage of daily workload: 5%
- Average salary: £16,000 per year or £61.50 per day
- **This means that the value *to the business* of this activity is £800 per year.**

By a combination of self, peer and management assessment you may identify the effectiveness of an individual in use of these skills. This should be based on a set of clear competencies (more on this in later steps – including a really useful free tool for mapping competencies).

From this, you may have determined that your receptionist is achieving 4/10, or 40% effectiveness.

Now this can be turned into a financial position:

Currently we pay £800 per year for this skill and the receptionist is performing to the value of 40% of that = £320. This means we are losing £480 in potential value.

If you can then measure effectiveness AFTER the training, you may see that with the new learning your receptionist has increased skills to 7/10, or 70% effectiveness.

This means that of the £800 you are paying a year for this skill you have increased the value from £320 per year to £560 per year. This is an increase in value from the investment of £240 per year.

Powerful stuff!

- ROI Thinking (taking in the wider picture)

The difference between ROI thinking and ROI analysis is that you apply a general appreciation of what you know to the wider picture in ROI Thinking; rather than having to count everything.

Analysis requires numbers in and numbers out; ROI thinking requires an approach to everything based on wider implications of value for money. In other words, you can justify your decisions based upon generalised ideas and accepted concepts.

The better skilled, the less the skill is needed

To use the doctor's receptionist example: We could say that it is an accepted principle that the receptionist will offer us better value for money in his or her role if s/he can deal with difficult and aggressive patients; especially if we have some measure or awareness of how often this may occur.

However, in using this thinking we may begin to realise that the better skilled the receptionist is, the less likely aggression will occur in the first place. We can therefore suggest that the more skilled the receptionist is the less likely he or she will require the skill.

To put this in context: Using an example from The Black Swan by Nassim Nicholas Taleb:

An airline was presented with the option of self-sealing bullet proof doors between passengers and pilots. The cost of installation was high and not considered viable.

In the wake of 9.11 this decision NOT to act and change the doors would seem like a terrible decision. But if the doors had been changed, 9.11 would not have taken place (not in the same way, at least) and we may never have known the true benefit. We are wise after the event.

When an event does not happen we cannot measure the benefit of its prevention!

ROI Thinking: using creativity to map potential

ROI Thinking requires you to use your creativity to consider where the potential benefits could be, and the potential measures that would be appropriate, without always having to actually apply them.

In our receptionist example, we can use ROI thinking to present to our employers that the reduction in distraction from aggressive patients, the improvement in patient relations and the reduction in time spent dealing with difficult patients will give us benefit in terms of using the receptionists' skills in other administration, marketing or patient relationship building tasks. We can begin to make a good business case for a good return on investment by relating the opportunities offered to potential income, savings or efficiency.

STEP 5 ACTION PLAN: MAKING PEOPLE A RETURN ON INVESTMENT

Do some ROI thinking and identify the areas in which people could make a difference and support the achievement of the Vision.

STEP 6: The caviar of measurements: ROE

- **Develop your Return on Expectations (ROE) approach**
- **Overview and principles of Kirkpatrick Model**

In order to do this you will need to use the Kirkpatrick model, something I have been using with my clients from the beginning.

Overview of the Kirkpatrick Model of Evaluation

The Kirkpatrick Model is a globally recognised method of evaluating training. It provides a framework for my evaluation process.

Key Principles of the Kirkpatrick Model	
a) The end is the beginning	"...begin with the desired results and then determine what behaviour is required to accomplish them..."
b) Return on Expectations (ROE)	"...the ultimate indicator of value..."
c) Business partnership to achieve ROE	"A positive relationship between training provider and client to achieve the best results."

Broadly speaking, evaluation using the Kirkpatrick Model increases in both complexity and investment through the 4 Levels.

The Kirkpatrick Model 4 Levels
Level 1: Reaction The simplest evaluation occurs at Level 1: Reaction. Delegates' 'reactions' to the training are assessed, usually using responses on post-training feedback sheets. A score of 90% or below would merit further investigation and follow up.
Level 2: Learning Either using pre/post-tests or ratings scales, delegates' levels of learning before and after the training are assessed. Research carried out by Dr Brent Peterson (Columbia University 2004) states that the actual training event contributes 24% towards learning (pre-work and follow-up contributing 26% and 50% respectively). Therefore a score of 25% or above at Level 2 would indicate greater than average effectiveness at this level.
Level 3: Behaviour Level 3 sees a jump in terms of both complexity and investment. Synergy use post-training coaching sessions to both support delegates in implementing their learning (changing their behaviour) and in gathering evidence to support the assessment.
Level 4: Results Level 4 is where 'the end is the beginning' is key. At the very beginning of the training process, *the end outcome was specified in the form of a behavioural competency. At Level 4 we analyse evidence gathered both during the training and coaching sessions to determine whether delegates have achieved the overall competency.*

STEP 6 ACTION PLAN: DEVELOP YOUR ROE APPROACH

Note down your ideal end results in terms of expectation.

STEP 7: Vision -> Action: FAST

- **Vision - Decision - Passion – Action**
- **Are you ready to push for change?**
- **Free tool! Find out your change personality**
- **Kotter's 8 Steps to Successful Change**

Having completed Steps 5 and 6, you've now got an idea of how to approach the concepts of ROI and ROE. Next up is reviewing the process of change – as change is absolutely essential to moving the business forward and implementing your plans.

Vision - Decision - Passion - Action

I run mentoring programmes about this approach for people in all aspects of business, so in a nutshell I will put to you what you need to do in order to start moving your business towards change.

Vision → Decision: stop time-wasting by embracing fire-fighting

Many Learning and Development professionals do not realise the difficulty or the time wasting that goes on between getting from vision to decision. It is easy to get embroiled in the next urgent topic, to get pulled away to deal with a difficulty somewhere, and to find that the overall process, the whole picture is being distorted by fire-fighting.

Fire-fighting is extremely undermining to proper, careful planning, and good quality skills development. What tends to happen is that the most difficult and poor performing employees, and the most challenging and high achieving employees get the maximum attention. The trouble is, these are usually between 20 - 40% of your total workforce. The remaining 60 - 80% are felt to flounder or struggle, and get on as best as they can.

All because of fire-fighting.

Christmas happens every year!

It is essential to remember that planning must include time for putting out fires - just as Christmas is not an emergency each year (if you celebrate it you are likely to do so every year and so you are likely to need extra funds every year!) so dealing with the 20% of your staff is a natural part of your working life. However, you must still ensure that the 80% are catered for if you are to create real value in the business - not only in terms of those employees, but also in terms of your own position, and your ability to apply good quality decisions and implement them, even when other pressures are upon you.

Are you ready to push for change? Ready, steady, go!

You may need to think about the essential changes you need to make in your own life and thinking before you consider going further. I have developed a simple questionnaire/profile in for this: *Ready, Steady, Go...?* Try it now, and see if you're ready to push for change!

Essential change is the necessity to alter your current working practices in order to be able to create a difference in your business or organisation.

Questionnaire: Ready, Steady, Go...?

Answer the questions, then add up the total 'yes', 'no' and 'don't know' answers in the boxes below.

1	Do you feel your life is out of control?	Yes / No / Don't Know
2	Do you frequently feel harassed?	Yes / No / Don't Know
3	Are you worried about what is happening at work without you?	Yes / No / Don't Know
4	Do you get flashes of panic about tasks you need to complete that you may forget/have forgotten?	Yes / No / Don't Know
5	Does this happen often?	Yes / No / Don't Know
6	Do you find planning too time consuming to carry out at all?	Yes / No / Don't Know
7	Do you find it difficult to complete a planning activity due to interruptions?	Yes / No / Don't Know
8	Do you find yourself resenting planning time because it prevents you from getting on with practical tasks?	Yes / No / Don't Know
9	Do you spend most days looking for information that is not close to hand or easy to locate?	Yes / No / Don't Know
10	Do you wish you were more successful?	Yes / No / Don't Know
11	Do you feel relaxed right now?	Yes / No / Don't Know
12	Are you happy to have left your work behind for the day?	Yes / No / Don't Know
13	Do you achieve what you want in life?	Yes / No / Don't Know
14	Are you able to relax about the work you have to do?	Yes / No / Don't Know
15	Do people tend to be supportive and helpful to you?	Yes / No / Don't Know
16	Do you know exactly what you want to achieve in the next week?	Yes / No / Don't Know
17	Do you know exactly what you want to achieve in the next year?	Yes / No / Don't Know
18	Do you have a clear picture of what it means to you to be a success?	Yes / No / Don't Know
19	Are you satisfied with your achievements?	Yes / No / Don't Know
20	Do you feel you have time to enjoy your life?	Yes / No / Don't Know

Add up your score.

Total 'yes' (A)	Total 'no' (B)	Total 'don't know' (C)

If you had more As than Bs... Your answers were more negative than positive

If you had more Bs than As... your answers were more positive than negative

Reflect on the answers you gave.

- What are your impressions from it?
- How do you feel about it?
- How effective do you feel you are at the moment?
- Are there aspects of your life you would like to change?

Free tool! Find out your change personality...

Find out your change personality – use my Psimplometric Profiling Tool™, free!

I developed Psimplometric Profiling Tools™ as an aid to engage learners – everyone loves learning about themselves! They provide a simple psychometric profile, showing the user how they perceive themselves at any given point in time. There are lots more covering a range of subjects available – email me for more information, hello@isynergizelife.com

As a special gift to 28 Steps readers, I'm offering the profile "Change Personality" totally free of charge. Usage is totally unlimited!

Answer the questions honestly, and the tool will give you an insight into your own change personality. Are you a Mutable, always looking for new things, or a Cardinal, who likes to consolidate? Are you an Ultra Cardinal, who is resistant to change or an Ultra Mutable who has to continually change in order to survive?

Try it - and see if you are ready to push for change!

READER FREEBIE! What's Your Change Personality?>
www.isynergizelife.com/28Steps/iSL_Change.xls
Download is an MS Excel file – you will need MS Excel installed on your device.

Kotter's 8 Steps to Successful Change

1. Establish a sense of urgency
2. Create a guiding coalition
3. Develop a clear and shared vision
4. Communicate the vision
5. Empower people to act on the vision
6. Create short term wins
7. Consolidate and build on the gains
8. Institutionalise the change

Explore iSynergizeLife.com for courses on Change

"Making Change Psychologically Compelling" covers everything above, and is one of our starred courses! We run it publicly from time to time – check http://www.iSynergizelife.com for details of upcoming events.

STEP 7 ACTION PLAN: IDENTIFY ESSENTIAL CHANGE

Are you ready to implement new plans and strategies? Reflect on your answers to the Ready, Steady, Go..? Questionnaire

CHAPTER 3: Fix the Wonky!
Introducing Steps 8 and 9

Edward De Bono describes the way in which we think and orientate ourselves as our polarity - we tend to be metaphorically p(' ˙ ' in a set direction.

It is as though we have a direction in mind in our life and we are looking in that direction. The trouble is, we can all have a different polarity, and so like a whole load of wonky compasses we all point in different directions. This is not helpful when you are all part of one organisation!

STEP 8: What has culture got to do with vision?

- **The value of a mutually agreed vision**
- **Cultural implications**

The value of a mutually agreed vision

We are never all going to be fully geared up and pointing in exactly the same direction like a set of true compasses. BUT engaging people in orientating themselves somewhat towards the same goal is essential for the business to develop and perform.

First we need to recognise that, as de Bono described, we all tend to be polarised in a set direction – and that these directions may be different. Then we need to work with this, to agree a forward vision; a direction for ALL to be moving towards.

Your role is VITAL in carefully helping stakeholders and business owners/employers to recognise the value of a mutually agreed forward vision.

Cultural implications

One overlooked aspect of orientating everyone towards the same goal is the problem of culture.

All organisations have cultures that create implications to the way in which they work, and understanding and becoming immersed in the culture is essential to the Learning and Development professional.

Charles Handy identified four key cultural types: Role Culture, Task Culture; Club Culture and Existential Culture. Your starting point should be to get a handle on the type of business you are in, because frequently the training department is a Task Culture, but the rest of the organisation may not be! This means that you may have difficulties trying to sell your ideas as they just create a cultural clash for some of the people in the business - often the owners or employers.

For this reason you must ensure that you carefully match the business's priorities to the solution you are offering. We recommend the organisational profile grid of Cameron and Quinn which measures the degree of flexibility, discretion and dynamism against stability, order and control on one axis, and the degree to which the organisation is internally or externally focussed on the other axis. Otherwise, contact me for one of my culture questionnaires and I send it free of charge."

In terms of the areas of need that you must investigate, we will look into that later on.

STEP 8 ACTION PLAN: WHAT IMPLICATIONS DOES YOUR CULTURE HAVE FOR THE VISION?

Carry out a culture questionnaire to ensure you are pitching your programme effectively.

STEP 9: Planning analysis – skills and people needs

- **Planning analysis in terms of skills or people needs**
- **Why it just won't work**
- **Bigger isn't better**
- **Speed is of the essence**

Planning analysis in terms of skills or people needs

Here, again, you can carry this part of the task out quite simply. However, this stage is often the   most   laborious   and   drawn   out of   all.........

I have watched organisations taking months and even years to design, send out and then process the results of their needs analysis.

By the time you have a good picture of what you need, guess what? A large proportion of your staff and environmental conditions have changed.

This is a major problem in Learning and Development! The professionals are trying to carry out static tactics in a changing environment.

It just won't work.

There are two key issues that need to be dealt with here:

- Bigger isn't better
- Speed is of the essence

Bigger isn't better

In other words that MASSIVE questionnaire is just not going to give you all you hope for, for two reasons.

You may never even get it back!

It assumes that the people you are asking know precisely what they don't know.

And how likely is it that people know what they don't know? The whole point is they don't know it! Let me explain a bit more...

- We know what we know;
- And we know some of what we don't know;
- But there is a massive amount of information that we don't know that we don't know;
- And so we can't evaluate its importance or relevance to us!

So I suggest that global questions are better than specific. Ask people in management positions if they feel comfortable:

- Giving praise - does it improve performance?
- Carrying out a reprimand - does it improve performance?

If the answers you get suggest that people not only feel uncomfortable about reprimand, but they also do not see it as useful, this is where you have to get BRAVE, and realise that you simply MUST include this in the development programme.

Too often, the needs analysis process becomes a preference process: what the delegate wants the delegate gets.

Instead, you need to work out first what they NEED and then decide how you are going to SELL them on it.

An excellent question you can ask is: "What is your number 1 most pressing challenge with...."

You could gain an enormous and instant insight if you used that question alone and then added three or four areas such as:

- In managing people
- In your own personal effectiveness
- In dealing with clients
- In achieving profitability

Please do not get blinded into thinking that you will demonstrate real value to your organisation by the pure brilliance and detail of your questionnaire. Sorry!

Your business will measure you against your success in improving business performance, not on the beauty of your survey.

Get it completed and provide feedback and a plan for moving forward - that will impress.

Four completed, returned questions are better than 100 uncompleted and unreturned questionnaires - half a loaf is better than no loaf at all!

Speed is of the essence.

There are two things you need from your survey:

- It is in date by the time you process it – returns must be the same day you send it
- It will automatically provide you with data – just very raw data at this stage

Bear in mind: you will not be able to perfect your learning and development offering before you begin carrying out your programme - you will need to take a Kaisen approach and work on a process of continual development - which will mean a perpetual state of transformational thinking (always being prepared to alter your point of view).

Management development is a continual process of evolution and adaptation - you will never get it right first time, but on the other hand, in getting it wrong you can be making progress.

In fact I would go as far as to say, that when you find the bits that don't work you are in a very strong position to better understand and develop what will.

The whole thing of stuff not working first time is all part of the game you are in, and your ability to manage that is what will make you stand out, impress and build the profile of your department and of yourself as an effective professional.

There is no other part of the business that can afford to wait for as long as HR *thinks* it can wait before it acts.

When the market changes, your marketers get cracking and start developing and releasing their newly developed products. In fact, they are usually anticipating future trends in readiness.

When the business is losing money, the finance department do not take a year to ask everyone what should be done - you usually are told very quickly that budgets will be held or spending frozen.

So remember, speed is of the essence, and get your programme started within 28 days!

Furthermore, apart from those off sick or on holiday etc. I would not count any questionnaires that do not get returned within the time period you specify.

One good way to get your surveys back quickly is to make them urgent and reward return.

For example, a free I-tunes download if the survey is returned by the end of the day; or for the first 20 returned.

So your email would say that they get rewarded if they get the survey back quickly and lose out on having their opinion heard if they do not.

You will be surprised what a little urgency, a manageably short questionnaire and a little reward can do!

STEP 9 ACTION PLAN: PLANNING ANALYSIS IN TERMS OF SKILLS OR PEOPLE NEEDS

Investigate and set up a survey system in readiness for your key questions.

Chapter 4: Solve the Problem of Delegates' Estimation

Steps 10- 13

How brainstorming isn't the way to start

One of the things that has become obvious to me through my years in this profession is how difficult it can be to look at such a large topic as management development and know where one should start.

Often it begins with lots of brainstorming, and people bringing in what they think from past experience, from new research, from the media and from listening to various people in the organisation.

Well, this is not a good way to go about this process. Creativity is best used when you want to explore ways of delivering, because this is where you will get your real value; by engaging the delegates in their learning.

It is not the best use of time or creativity to use your brains re-inventing the wheel.

Balancing the areas of management development

In essence, I have figured that there are four key areas of development in management:

- Managing yourself (Personal Effectiveness)
- Managing others (People Management)

- Managing the business (Business Strategy)
- Managing the client

There is no doubt that a good manager will have a good balance of all of these (although the client management aspect is not necessarily relevant to all).

Before you start thinking about courses and competencies you need to consider these three major topic headings and ask some very simple questions regarding the business and how important each of these are to it. You can commence this with your Global Needs Analysis, which leads us nicely into Step 10.

STEP 10: The Global Needs Analysis

- **Use ROI Thinking to prioritise**
- **The Prioritising Challenge**

Use ROI Thinking to prioritise

Using ROI thinking - what do you think the overall level of skill is in each area? This will only give you an estimate of your needs.

What is your estimation of the level of importance to the business? By combining this with the above you can begin to see whether you need to be thinking about this major topic area as a priority, or as an immediate and pressing need, or an urgency which will require a fire fighting approach. Please see figure opposite - this is a picture of my Needs Analyst which drills down into each of the areas, but commences with a simple analysis of where you need to put your attention.

The Prioritising Challenge

It can sometimes seem that EVERYTHING is a priority; EVERYTHING is an immediate and pressing need. EVERYTHING is a fire that needs to be extinguished. We all know this SIMPLY ISN'T TRUE!

We also all know that working out which skills need addressing first is definitely easier said than done. This is the Prioritising Challenge.

My Needs Analyst is such an incredibly powerful tool that helps you meet the prioritising challenge. Like magic, it turns your answers into a profile that shows you where, and on what you need to be focussing your attention.

Interested? As a 28 Steps reader, my Needs Analyst is FREE!
www.isynergizelife.com/28steps/NA.html

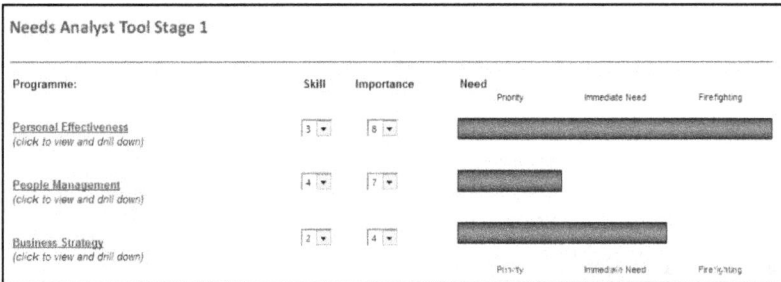

Needs Analyst Tool Stage 1						
Programme:	Skill	Importance	Need			
			Priority	Immediate Need	Firefighting
Personal Effectiveness (click to view and drill down)	3	8				
People Management (click to view and drill down)	4	7				
Business Strategy (click to view and drill down)	2	4				
			Priority	Immediate Need	Firefighting

STEP 10 ACTION PLAN: Step 10 - GLOBAL NEEDS ANALYSIS

Use your understanding of the business's needs to carry out a broad based analysis of what you will need.

STEP 11: Approaching the Design of Your Analysis

- **Set menu, or a la carte?**
- **It all boils down to choice or need.**

Set menu, or a la carte?

How you go about assessing individuals will depend upon your business's method of working, or your agreed approach to management development, which may be either:

- Set Menu Style: assess skills and provide accordingly - so that individuals can meet the business needs and priorities;
- Or a la Carte: allow delegates to choose what courses they would like to attend.

Personally, I prefer the set menu: to assess what the business needs, and provide on that basis. I know some L&D professionals believe that they will not achieve buy-in, particularly if the programme is, to a greater or lesser extent, optional. I do not think that should be a factor in decision making at this time. The business needs should come first, and the creativity of the L&D team comes into play in the internal marketing of the programme - more on that later.

It all boils down to choice or need.

First then, you need to make a decision about how you are going to go about this. Are you Set Menu, or a la Carte? Are you offering a business *needs* orientated programme, or a delegate-*chosen* programme?

Clearly, this decision will be made with the major stakeholder – or, it will already be a part of policy. But it is in this type of decision that you can demonstrate your value to the business. Your seniors are going to want to be able to justify your role, and L&D, not just as a necessary evil but as a REAL business benefit. So I think you can see why I favour the Business Needs approach.

STEP 11 ACTION PLAN: APPROACHING THE DESIGN OF YOUR ANALYSIS

Decide if you will:

- Assess skills and provide accordingly - so that individuals can meet the business needs and priorities
- Allow delegates to choose what courses they would like to attend.

STEP 12: I'm AMAZING!! Accounting for Learning Curve Bias

- The killer combination for reviewing needs
- The Learning Curve
- The role of morale
- Relating the LC to reality

The killer combination for reviewing needs

When I review the needs of employees there is one key thing that I want to know before I do anything more: where are they on the learning curve?

Then I want to find out where they are in terms of their Skills, Attitudes and Behaviours.

This combination is important. In fact, it is a killer combination. Here's why: if you ask an individual about their level of skill, they will answer you according to where they perceive their skill to be, and this may not reflect reality. So, you combine it with their level on the learning curve, and THINK: how could their position on the learning curve be affecting the responses they give?

The Learning Curve

We have all heard about the learning curve and use it as a metaphor, but here I want to look at it in terms of the *way in which we learn new skills*.

The best way to understand it is to use an analogy that we can relate to. I usually like to use the analogy of learning to drive a car, because it is quite meaningful to many people.

If you are a driver, then think back to the days before you could drive. It is quite likely that you looked upon the prospect of driving with great excitement, perhaps you saw your Granny or Granddad drive and thought, well, if they can do it, then I MUST be able to - yes, all this amid the delightful arrogance of youth! On the other hand, you may have been somewhat nervous about the prospect.

However, the key issue at this point is that you have had no experience and so "you don't know what you don't know". The learner at this stage is called "unconsciously incompetent" - unconscious, because they have no awareness as yet, and incompetent as they have no skill.

Once the learner gets behind the wheel the task in hand can seem outrageously impossible. Co-ordination, which seems so easy to others, suddenly feels like trying to pat your head and rub your stomach at the same time - only worse. At this stage the learner discovers that there is a lot he or she doesn't know - "I now know what I don't know - and it's a lot!" So at this stage we describe the learner as "consciously incompetent" - in other words, their incompetence has come into their awareness in graphic terms. Now this stage does not relate to how we feel about what we know, only the facts of our knowledge - what I mean is, the learner may think he has discovered that he knows nothing, but in fact he has learnt a lot, he has learnt what he needs to know. So this is a major and necessary move up the learning curve, albeit an uncomfortable one.

After some time of instruction and practice we get to a point where we can do the task, we can drive, but only if we concentrate very hard. This is where we are "consciously competent" - i.e. I can do it when I think about it. At this stage we find distractions extremely difficult to deal with, we need time to contemplate and think, and we need to take things fairly slowly.

After a while, we find that we are able to drive without really thinking about it. It becomes "automatic".

This is when we become "unconsciously competent" - in that our competence is embedded into our behaviours and we no longer need to think consciously about what we are doing. We just do it.

The Learning Curve

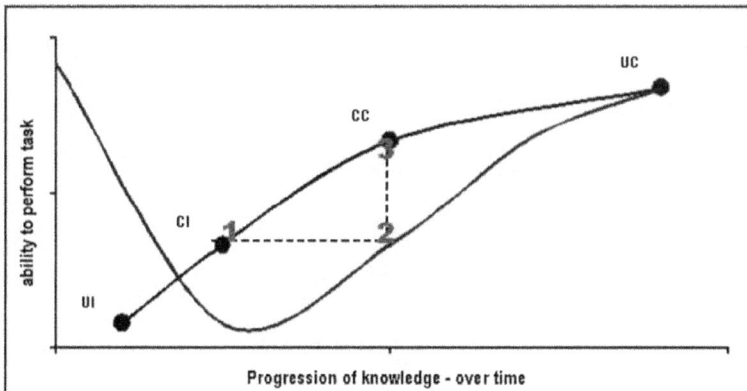

The Learning Curve chart showing ability to perform task (vertical axis) against Progression of knowledge - over time (horizontal axis), with points UI, CI, CC, UC and numbered markers 1, 2, 3.

The role of morale

This knowledge of the learning curve is extremely helpful for learners and trainers alike. But there is an important additional dimension; and that is the role of morale.

When we start on a new task or a new job we are often enthusiastic and, if we have seen people performing in this task competently we may think that it will be fairly easy. This is when we are "unconsciously incompetent".

Of course, when we discover how much more there is to the task, when we become "consciously incompetent" our morale is likely to drop like a stone.

Furthermore, it tends to lag behind for a while, even when our skills improve. This means the way in which we perceive our skills are affected by our position on the learning curve, more than by reality. If you look at the chart you will see that the "morale" curve dips while the learning curve rises. The morale curve (which represents our perception of our skill level) can give a very false impression.

Relating the Learning Curve to reality

Now think about this with relation to management development. People coming in at entry level are likely to rate their skills higher than they may be in reality, simply because they have not actually applied these to any great extent - they may be "unconsciously incompetent".

A person at the intermediate level may rate themselves lower on skills than they are in reality. And a senior level and highly competent manager will, surprisingly enough, often be keen to gain additional or refresher skills. So your needs analysis could look like this:

RELATING THE LEARNING CURVE TO REALITY	
ACTUAL management level	PERCEIVED level from Needs Analysis
Entry level manager	Highest skill set
Intermediate level manager	Low level skill set
Senior level manager	Lowest level skill set

So to recap: the learning curve bias can alter peoples' perceptions of their knowledge, skills and abilities. As L&D Professionals, we must be aware of this, and account for it.

STEP 12 ACTION PLAN: ACCOUNTING FOR LEARNING CURVE BIAS

Ensure you are aware of how perceived skills levels will affect your result.

STEP 13: Strip out bias: true learning curve positions

- **Creating a questionnaire to position delegates on the Learning Curve**
- **Example Learning Curve Question**

Creating a questionnaire to position delegates on the Learning Curve

In Step 12 we reviewed the Learning Curve. Hopefully, this helped make it clear that you will need to start by asking questions that will give you a handle on where delegates are on the learning curve. This really isn't as onerous as it sounds…

- If they are likely to be at the bottom (but think they are at the top) you will not need to ask any skills questions at all. They should go into the programme at entry level.
- If they demonstrate experience but lack confidence - then they will need to enter the programme at the intermediate level, and may want to select their courses they feel they could most benefit from.
- If they demonstrate a good level of experience, show a reasonable amount of skill, but desire improvement, then they may be most appropriate for a senior level programme.

You see, you may not need to ask anything like the amount you thought you would!

Example Learning Curve Question

1) Have you experienced managing others in this organisation?
   (This question guides us on where they may be on the learning curve).

   If so, is your experience:

   A. Carried out full projects from beginning to end including evaluation of team members contributions and performance and fully confident. ***Potentially a senior level intake***
   B. Have not carried out projects, but feel fairly / very confident about tackling it. ***Potentially junior/entry level intake***
   C. Carried out projects but still believe could learn more and develop some skills (perhaps specific skills). ***Potentially intermediate level intake***
   D. Not carried out projects and do not feel very confident. ***Potentially junior/entry level intake*** .

2) How confident do you feel about moving into a management role and having to supervise and manage colleagues:
   A. Not confident at all
   B. Lack confidence about some aspects
   C. Fairly Confident
   D. Very confident

Now, bear in mind, that the answers you receive are only based upon the PERCEPTION of the employee. Perhaps only a 360 degree questionnaire will give you a complete and thorough view.

That is why you may have to use **judgement** and **anecdotal evidence** to shape and develop the actual outcomes. For example, if the majority of employees said that they were feeling confident, but you suspected that this did not necessarily add up with your experience or observations, you will need to weight the question accordingly.

So, for example:

- 80% perceived that they felt fairly or very confident.
- Our observations from anecdotal evidence suggests this perception may not be in line with reality and experience. Therefore, it is considered that a high anticipated level of confidence in this area may be related stage one of the learning curve.

The answers you will get to your questions will depend greatly upon this information.

STEP 13 ACTION PLAN: CREATE A QUESTIONNAIRE TO DETERMINE THE DELEGATE STAGE OF DEVELOPMENT ON THE LEARNING CURVE

Plan your questionnaire to take perceptions into account.

Chapter 5: Designing for People Development

Steps 14-15

Putting the questions to the delegates

Now you have a grasp on how you are going to approach assessing needs, this is the point where you have to exercise your professional judgement.

Every organisation believes themselves to have absolutely unique needs, and it is true that I have never carried out the same management development programme for two businesses. However, there is also some truth that the overall competencies that are required in business will be the same, it's just that your business may not need them all - or that your business may prioritise differently and have different skills levels.

Have confidence, and courage!

You need to have the confidence and courage of your convictions here, because, it is at this point that your organisation are benefitting from the skill, experience and knowledge that you bring to the business.

My experience of working with HR and Learning and Development Professionals has taught me that, almost without exception, these are a really friendly, supportive, open minded and generally nice bunch of people.

These qualities also make L&D people good listeners, interested in solving people problems, and excellent at taking on and responding to different points of view.

In their roles, therefore, these people are good at listening and noticing what is happening, and are highly motivated to support individuals as well as teams. It may feel quite alien for an L&D person to put their own point of view across, and to do so quite forcibly.

To be honest, if it comes down to supporting and protecting their people, they will fight tooth and nail, but I think that these people have spent so much time and energy on doing just that, in gaining respect for their profession, that there is almost an apologetic atmosphere in some businesses where L&D people believe that their justification for their role can be seen in the quality of their work - and this can sometimes result in very complex pieces of analysis.

I have said this before, and will not apologise for repeating it here: You will be judged on your results. And, you must, (if you do not already believe this, then you need to start now) recognise that it is your professional judgement and ability to implement rapidly that will save your job and everyone else's.

To be frank, I would not be in the business of people development if I didn't totally believe that people are the difference between business success and failure.

For this reason I have total respect for those people who work in developing, supporting and maintaining the well-being of a business's employees.

A tool to guide you

The key link between the initial assessment of the business need and the delegate needs analysis is the judgement of performance.

On the other hand, the whole area of assessing needs is a minefield, and so I have put together, over many years, a simple process to help you. I hope this will allow my professional colleagues and clients to focus on what they do best; communicating, thinking creatively, focussing on the business needs and supporting the workforce.

STEP 14: Management ABS: are they being sucked in?

- Management ABS – Attitudes, Behaviours and Skills
- Focus on essential ABS
- Ask testing questions
- Trade secret alert!

Management ABS – Attitudes, Behaviours and Skills

When you start thinking about drilling down into the actual specific needs of individuals, you should be thinking about Attitudes Behaviours and Skills:

Attitudes - how they approach it

Behaviours - what they actually do

Skills - how they apply knowledge to action

Again, if you set up a simple questionnaire asking what participants are skilful in, you are not likely to get the answers that will really help your assessment of their skills. People can tend to 'suck in' their ABS, perhaps not give a true picture of their needs. This is not always intentional.

Focus on essential ABS

My preferred approach here is to focus on Attitudes Behaviours and Skills that relate to two essential competency areas: managing self, and managing others.

Why? Because you extrapolate information that can inform other areas - including client communication and business strategy - from these two essential competencies.

I also think that you can much more easily determine if someone feels they have adequate skills in, for example, finance, by simply asking - because at a strategic level there are quite a few areas that are fairly technical, rather than soft skill. The same with sales skills, for example - it is fairly easy to see if someone is successful or not, and a good sales manager will be able to quickly identify at which stage the sales person may need additional support.

Ask testing questions

In assessing attitudes, behaviour and skills I have taken the view that it is most effective to ask questions that actually test the real understanding of the delegate.

In my questionnaire I use a number of pairs of questions, one of which will mark highly as "always" and one that marks highly at "never". A point to note is that I don't necessary give top marks for "always" as it is an unrealistic statement; i.e. it is unlikely that anyone would be able to claim that "I *always* manage my time fairly".

TRADE SECRET ALERT!

I prefer to reward honesty and flexibility. So, if someone answered always and never in all the "right" places, they wouldn't necessarily score as highly as someone who says "frequently" or "seldom". This is a trade secret, so please keep it to yourself. I might add, I never disclose to which questions this applies!!

Honesty = excellence

A manager who is able to be honest in their assessment of themselves is, by that ability alone, demonstrating excellent levels of self-perception, and therefore most likely to be capable of individual reflection and self-improvement.

My questions are set up so that if a delegate answers in habituation, or if they answer what they think is the right answer it will create conflict and they will lose marks on that question. This gives me a clearer picture of where they may actually require some specific and clear support and development - and that is, after all, the whole point of this exercise.

The image below shows some example questions from my Attitudes/Behaviours/Skills Questionnaire. I consider the following areas:

- Communication (Managing Self)
- Team work (Managing Self)
- Relationships (Managing Self and Managing Others)
- Management (Managing Others)
- Leadership (Managing Others)

This questionnaire takes into account relevant experience, and the design is such that it takes into account the bias that may be expressed as a result of the position of the delegate on the learning curve.

ATTITUDES/BEHAVIOURS/SKILLS QUESTIONNAIRE					
Leadership	Always	Often	Occasionally	Seldom	Never
Do you manage your team fairly?					
When performance is poor do you prefer to avoid reprimanding staff?					
Does the motivation of your staff affect the team's outputs/productivity?					
How often do you need to address problems of morale?					
Do you take responsibility for your teams' performance?					
Do you pass full accountability on to your staff when you delegate to them?					
Do you like to balance a nurturing and directing approach to management?					
Do you have a standard management method for all situations?					
Can you demonstrate that your people are fulfilling your potential?					
Do you have difficulty recognising the reasons for poor performance in your staff?					

STEP 14 ACTION PLAN: DESIGN YOUR NEEDS ANALYSIS QUESTIONNAIRE

Design your Needs Analysis Questionnaire.

Ensure your questionnaire:

- Assesses attitude, behaviours and skills
- Can identify potential conflict or habituation

STEP 15: Building the questionnaire at three levels

- **Top tips for building your needs analysis questionnaire**
- **Drilling into the competencies – secret shortcut alert!**

Top tips for building your needs analysis questionnaire

- Keep the number of questions to a minimum - no more than can be answered in 3 minutes maximum.
- Ensure you cover the global areas as required (managing self, managing others, managing the business, managing clients)
- Ask yes, no (or don't know if you must) questions or provide multiple choice.
- Ensure your questions focus on the areas of need you have identified - don't ask everything - just ask what you need to know *right now*. For example, if your high priority is self-management, then focus more delegate energy on this initially.
- Remember, that short and sweet needs analysis can be repeated again and again, because they take little effort from the delegate, and little time for the L&D department. One massive questionnaire that may get things wrong, after months of setting up and implementing is less useful than lots of little ones, which may be updated and altered regularly, and that provide instant results.
- Other things may arise as you begin your programme - that is not a failure of planning, it is normal.

My simple step by step process enables you to very quickly develop an effective needs analysis – and from there leap into a well thought through management development plan, and escalate your company profits and your reputation to great heights.

The diagram shows the three tiers I set for my analysis. This can actually guide you to which of the three levels of management development programme each delegate should enter.

Your programme of development will be unique, specific, answer needs and be developed from start to finish in 28 Steps!

Management Development Programme: THREE LEVELS

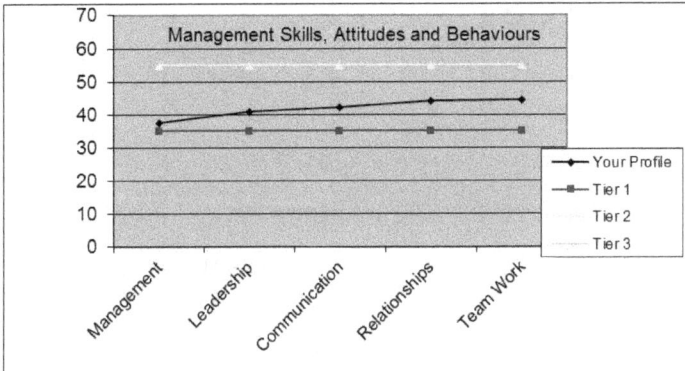

Drilling into the competencies – secret shortcut alert!

Once you have prioritised basic needs, you can start to do the same in each area by drilling down into the major competencies. Then you can go further still and identify specific competencies you want your people to demonstrate.

Or… you could take a shortcut! My Needs Analyst does all this, and is easy, fast and simple to use. AND as a 28 Steps Subscriber, it's FREE!! Visit www.isynergizelife.com/28Steps/NA.html to download (uses MS Excel)

So if you want to get a full set of competencies in a day, then visit the web site and download the Needs Analyst. On the other hand, you can spend months and months re-inventing the wheel. The choice is yours!

I have spent years doing all this work for you - so take total advantage of me. I've done all this so you don't have to.

STEP 15 ACTION PLAN: BUILDING THE QUESTIONNAIRE AT THREE LEVELS

Remember:

- Cover global areas
- Only ask what you really need to know

Chapter 6: The key skills your people MUST have

Steps 16, 17 and 18

Pin it down: relate your plan to your framework

Once you have got an idea from your needs analysis you can then use your judgement to create a plan for your management development programme.

You then need to relate this to your company competency framework, or simply use the free Needs Analyst (visit www.isynergizelife.com/28Steps/NA.html) provided on my website.

Foundation skills: focussing on the self and personal effectiveness. This could be areas like communication, confidence.

People management skills: how we relate to and manage others. For example delegation, managing appraisals, giving feedback

Strategic management skills: how we lead, our vision, forward planning for the business. This could be areas like managing change, strategic planning.

The next three steps consider these key skill areas, and how to relate them to your framework.

STEP 16 – The essential foundation skills

- **Pin it down: relate your plan to your framework**
- **Focus on the essentials: SELF**

Focus on the essentials: SELF

The first stage in assessing competency and training needs is to consider the area of personal effectiveness. If an individual is unable to manage themselves then we can assume that they would probably be fairly ineffectual in managing others! So it is always sensible to begin with the self.

You can tackle and complete this task in a day if you use my free assessor. This takes each of the competency areas shown after Step 18 and further breaks them down into specific competencies.

STEP 16 ACTION PLAN: THE ESSENTIAL FOUNDATION SKILLS
Start by assessing personal effectiveness skills

STEP 17 – The essential people management skills

- **Identify people management competencies**
- **Remember the business!**

Identify people management competencies

As with Step 16, use my Needs Analyst! This enables you to identify the key people management competencies for your people. You can refer to the needs analysis to judge the level of skill in each area, although as you will see the needs analysis gives a broad picture of each area i.e. management, teamwork etc.

Remember the business!

Remember to input the business's requirements or priorities, and then feel confident about using your own judgement.

STEP 17 ACTION PLAN: THE ESSENTIAL PEOPLE MANAGEMENT SKILLS

Review how people work with their team.

STEP 18 – The essential strategic management skills

- **Identify strategic management competencies**
- **Something very important to remember during Steps 16, 17 and 18**

Identify strategic management competencies

Finally, you can identify the strategic management skills and some of the more technical skills such as marketing and finance using the free Needs Analyst available at http://www.isynergizelife.com/28Steps/NA.html

Something very important to remember during Steps 16, 17 and 18!

Your delegates may not know what they need to know - in fact, it is my experience from the training room that they usually do not. Therefore it is dangerous to leave out an element because no one requests it. **I will keep coming back to this point** - you must use **YOUR** knowledge, judgement and skill in identifying what would be a good and well-rounded management development programme for your company. Keep your focus on the business needs right up until the delivery - and the marketing of the delivery - begins.

Assessing foundation, managing self skills

Topic	Skill	Importance	Need (Priority — Immediate Need — Firefighting)		
New Management Role — The manager confidently moves into a management role	1	8	Priority	Immediate Need	Firefighting
Managing Self — The manager organises his/her workload and manages energy, priorities and emotions productively	4	6			
Communication — The manager communicates with confidence and persuasively	3	6			
Written Communication — The manager writes fluently and appropriately	4	8			
Planning — The manager creates effective plans	3	5			
Decision Making — The manager uses deduction and creativity to make solid, reasonable decisions	4	5			
Presentations — The manager presents to audiences confidently and impressively	2	2			
Work Life Balance — The manager maintains a healthy work/life balance	2	3	Priority	Immediate Need	Firefighting

Assessing people management skills

Topic	Skill	Importance	Need (Priority — Immediate Need — Firefighting)		
Confident Management — The manager confidently and assertively communicates and acts with peers, managers and staff	7	8	Priority	Immediate Need	Firefighting
Development and Delegation — The manager motivates and develops staff potential through effective delegation that responds to individual needs	5	9			
Teamwork — The manager effectively promotes teamwork among his/her team and in the wider organisation	7	8			
Recruitment — The manager identifies, selects and interviews the right person for the job	6	5			
Leadership — The manager is an inspiring and flexible leader of his/her team	4	4			
Managing Performance — The manager monitors, manages and motivates the team and individuals' performance over the short, medium and long term	3	7			
Managing Relationships — The manager effectively manages relationships with peers, managers and staff and clients	4	7	Priority	Immediate Need	Firefighting

Assessing business or strategic management skills

Topic	Skill	Importance	Need		
			Priority	Immediate Need	Firefighting
Managing Processes and Operations The manager manages operations through efficient and effective processes	1 ▼	1 ▼			►
Ethics in Business The manager carries out his/her role ethically, based upon a well-developed sense of integrity and fairness	7 ▼	4 ▼	████████		►
Change The manager positively embraces and manages change	2 ▼	8 ▼	██████████████████		►
Managing Marketing The manager strategically manages the marketing operation	5 ▼	8 ▼	██████████████		►
Managing Finance The manager carries out well-informed financial planning and analysis	8 ▼	8 ▼	████████		►
Managing Business Strategy The manager takes a strategic approach to managing and developing human resources	5 ▼	5 ▼	████████		►
Managing Well Being The manager has a healthy work/life balance that enables him/her to support the well being of others	3 ▼	10 ▼	██████████████████		►
			Priority	Immediate Need	Firefighting

STEP 18 ACTION PLAN: THE ESSENTIAL STRATEGIC MANAGEMENT SKILLS

Consider the way individuals engage with the business.

Chapter 7: Drilling for Victory

Steps 19 and 20

During Chapter 6 (The Key Skills Your People MUST Have) we looked at identifying overall competencies for the key skills areas:

- Foundation skills
- People management skills
- Strategic management skills – or managing the business

Steps 19 and 20 drill down even further, to set you up with strong evidence of your success. We look at what do you actually need your people to DO? What behaviours do you want them to demonstrate?

The most important thing is to decide which behaviour competencies to include, and what priority they take. Once you have this information, you can look at how you will *know* the delegate is demonstrating this behaviour – what evidence will prove there has actually been a change?

Again, my Needs Analyst tool provides an excellent short cut for you at both these Steps – use my hard work!

STEP 19 – Drilling to expansive success

- **Rating the major competencies**

Rating the major competencies

Each major competency area is rated in two terms:

1. Importance to the business
2. Level of skills the workforce demonstrate

Obviously, if you asked everyone to rate their own level of skills you would get a whole load of different answers, and they would probably be inaccurate.

So you fill this bit in yourself, or as a consensual team, based on the broad answers you have received to your survey from delegates, the broad answers you have received from the business stakeholders, senior managers etc and *your own judgement.*

Drill down into the competencies to identify the content of your course in terms of outcomes.

Drilling down: rating the major competencies

STAGE 3

| Change | Urgency | Return to Topic Analyst |
| The manager positively embraces and manages change | This area requires urgent and immediate attention | |

Order your priorities:
Read each competency and then check the box to select the course.
Once you have selected the courses put them in order by prioritising them (with 1 being top priority) - every course must have a different priority, i.e.1,2,3 etc.

Include?	Priority (1=first 3=last)	Course Title
☑	2	**Personal Change** The manager is aware of his/her own fears/insecurities and uses this knowledge to create personal change
☐		**Re-orientating People** The manager is sensitive to the reasons for fearing change, and responds flexibly
☑	1	**Managing Change** The manager prepares his/her team for change creating commitment from staff

STEP 19 ACTION PLAN: DRILLING TO EXPANSIVE SUCCESS

Assess the major competencies you need and their urgency: priority, immediate need, fire-fighting

STEP 20 – The success behaviours

- **What do you actually want them to DO?**
- **Don't get too detailed**
- **Remember the golden rule!**
- **Use key mission statements**
- **Happy sheets don't develop people; competencies do!**

What do you actually want them to DO?

This is where you begin to think about what you want your people to be able to DO.

Now, it would be an extremely time-consuming task to work out all of this if it had not already been done for you. If you have competencies, for your business, but do not have these expressed as DEMONSTRABLE competencies, then you have some options:

- You define ALL the specifics you want people to be able to do yourself.
- You use a template (a good option!)
- You take a global view, and allow the people developing the programmes to do all this hard work for you (which may end up being you, if it is not an external supplier).

Don't get too detailed

Again, you do not need to get too detailed.

You just need to be clear in your mind what you want the outcome to look like. I prefer to take a very broad view of this, it should be able to be expressed in a very few words, much like a mission statement.

Once you have that, you can ensure that the specifics of the course you choose will answer this,.

Remember the golden rule:

YOU DO NOT NEED TO MEASURE EVERYTHING!

Sorry for shouting, but it is so, so important that you really get this, because it will save you HOURS of gnashing and wailing trying to work out how you can demonstrate that someone is able to "think conceptually", or "be creative and flexible in their approach". These sort of things cannot be demonstrated through a simple demonstrable competency, it will require far more qualitative assessment.

Use key mission statements

I suggest you set yourself three key mission statements which say what the individual will be able to do when they finish the programme.

Use a Bloom's taxonomy for each tier or level of management development. An example is included. This is a broad example, but you should make it meaningful to your business. You can put in additional lines too, so that after the main mission, you may specify some other global competencies; such as "through use of financial information" or "uses assertive and supportive communication" etc.

Example of possible taxonomy for competencies		
Tier	Taxonomy	Example "mission statement" style of competency
Foundation	Understands, explores	The Delegate understands the key skills and how they should be applied in people management.
Intermediate	Analyse, explain , demonstrates	The delegate can explain and analyse different skills that they need to apply in effective management demonstrating the relevant competencies.
Advanced	Evaluate, justify, plan and carry out	The delegate evaluates and justifies their performance in managing people demonstrating relevant the competencies to a high standard.

Happy sheets don't develop people; competencies do!

I recommend that all the courses you run are related to demonstrable competencies. You can then use the course to assess the competency - even if it is only to check understanding.

As a business, you should be able to see if your people are performing in the way that you want them to. And this is strangely, often an area missing in L&D. I think that L&D professionals are so involved in the evolving needs of the business it is often difficult to complete a programme and tie up all the loose ends.

I also notice in some businesses that the post-course evaluation – often based on those wonderful happy sheets - becomes the key document after the training event. Don't get me wrong, evaluation IS very useful, but it does not, in itself, address the issues of delegates failing to develop competencies.

In fact, if you are not careful, it can be used as an excuse for delegates to abdicate responsibility for uncomfortable messages through advocating a "shoot the messenger" approach.

I will talk more about getting real meaning and useful information from course evaluation later.

STEP 20 ACTION PLAN: THE SUCCESS BEHAVIOURS

Turn your competencies into things people can actually do - don't try to assess everything.

Chapter 8: The Secret to Fast Tracking Success
Steps 21, 22 and 23

It is at this point that I am going to quote John Ruskin (1819 -1900):

"It's unwise to pay too much but it's unwise to pay too little. When you pay too much you lose a little money, that is all.

When you pay too little, you sometimes lose everything, because the thing you bought was incapable of doing the thing you bought it to do.

The common law of business balance prohibits paying a little and getting a lot. It can't be done.

If you deal with the lowest bidder, it's well to add something for the risk you run.

And if you do that, you will have enough to pay for something better!"

In this chapter I want to talk about how you use your budget, because, the fact is, you cannot get quality delivery for nothing. You just can't. And 100 years later, after John Ruskin, you still can't.

But you can box clever with your budget.

STEP 21 – Know the cost of everything, *AND* the value of everything

- **Stop wasting money!**
- **Complacency is a trap**
- **Don't panic – you're onto a winner**
- **Go against the grain for a moment – think of employees as equipment**

Stop wasting money!

Oscar Wilde said "The cynic knows *the price of everything and the value of nothing*". In Step 21 I want you to focus on the value of your provision. And most importantly, ensuring that your provision produces value.

Running a development programme is a waste of time and money if it doesn't produce a result for the business, and the business measures its results by the bottom line.

Every penny you invest of your budget needs to have a bottom line benefit to the business - directly, or, more likely, indirectly. But the important thing is, you must be thinking about this if you want to save your job and everybody else's, because if a business is to provide lots of wonderful benefits to its employees, job security, a happy and productive working atmosphere, the opportunity to succeed, positive and enjoyable challenges, guess what? It needs to be able to afford to.

And even if the board have not demanded that provision shows a bottom line benefit, YOU need to be doing so.

Complacency is a trap!

Constantly keep in your mind just why you are doing this. It should be to the mutual benefit of employees and employers - the employers can obviously take the view that it is enlightened self-interest on their part.

Do not fall into the trap of believing that because employers see intrinsic value in learning and development that they will continue to fund it when times get tight.

The business and its ability to make a profit will always come first. And quite right too, if it is going to survive – it's not much good to any of us if it fails.

Don't panic – you're onto a winner

The bit of good news here is, of course, that the single most important factor in the success of a business is its people. So we are onto a winner already.

If we can guide and steer those people to increased effectiveness, and prove that we have done so, why would the business want to lose such vital components?

So you need to start with your current investment in your employees. On a very basic and simple note, the average employee who commences with the firm on £25,00 per annum will cost the business £4million after 30 years' service.

So just think about your current staffing bill. If you had a piece of machinery that cost that much, what would you consider a good investment in its maintenance and repair per annum?

Go against the grain for a moment – think of employees as equipment

Your programmes are effectively the maintenance and repair of your employees.

If you invested such a huge sum of money in a piece of equipment, would you want to know how productive it was? What would you do if it was only working at 70% capacity? I'm sure you would get in an engineer to solve the problem and increase its productivity.

Well, it is quite common for employees to be operating at far less than 70% productivity. Furthermore, they often know it and would like to do something about it; and strangely this is most often true for the most experienced managers.

They do not realise it and cannot do anything about it when they are junior and inexperienced.

And the very experienced, effective managers frequently recognise that they, too, have areas that need tuning up. They may not always be the most senior, though!

So, ensure you get a breakdown of employment costs and salaries. You will need to know at least the average salary for your delegates; for example, an average salary at each level of your programme.

Even better is to have the actual salary. Later I will show you how you can use this information to provide bottom line ROI data for your board and senior managers.

Step 21 ACTION PLAN: KNOW THE COST OF EVERYTHING *AND* THE VALUE OF EVERYTHING

Get a breakdown of employment costs

Value each key skill area in terms of the percentage of time it requires or the percentage of importance to the business.

STEP 22 – Discover the secrets to quick victories

- **Where can you find quick victories?**
- **Simple + effective = success**
- **Happy delegates vs. change**

Where can you find quick victories?

The way you manage your budget should put emphasis on the areas that will give you the highest value results in the shortest time. There is no harm in going for quick victories. This does not only enhance your profile, it also increases morale among the workforce, can create real change quickly and result in genuine benefits to the bottom line.

I have made a list of the top subject areas for quick victories.

- Assertive Communication
- Proactive self management
- Presentation Skills
- Effective Feedback including Praise and Reprimand
- Team Leadership

- Delegation

These are actually key areas, and in themselves they can be quite broad, but it is the essential competencies that you should start with.

Simple + effective = success

Every time I have run the Praise and Reprimand course, even if it is just the very fundamental elements of it, I have achieved:

- Extremely challenged delegates
- Extremely satisfied delegates
- Highly motivated delegates
- Real changes in behaviours
- Real bottom line benefits to the business.
- Happy stakeholders

Praise and Reprimand is such a vital and key skill, and yet even top flight directors have difficulties with it. With a good programme that provides simple but effective strategies you are onto a winner.

So, the point here is that these are the areas where you can get real value. But it also means you must invest quite heavily.

It's tempting to think that because it's a small subject you can do it in a minimal amount of time. Not so.

For example, I have a unit of learning on Praise and Reprimand which, in essence is three hours. If you run this for three hours you will undoubtedly have some success and happy delegates.

Happy delegates vs. change

What you will not necessarily have is real CHANGE. Now, let's remind ourselves of ROI thinking. If we want a return on our investment we need to think what is going to create a REAL difference.

I usually find when I speak to delegates and L&D managers that they all agree on the following: If managers were able to correct behaviour that was not effective - without confrontation and conflict - the life of the business would be more pleasant and much more productive. The negative consequences of poor praise and reprimand have a corresponding, real and immediate *negative* effect on our business performance.

Your ROI thinking needs to take into account "negative consequences". In other words, what happens if we can't or if we don't.

This is ROI thinking in action. Start looking at "what if it doesn't work?" then ask, "How much better could we be if it does work?"

It doesn't end there though. Because, as I have said from the outset, for me, being in this line of work is about making a difference, not about running a course and then moving on.

I want every course I develop, run or recommend to make an improvement to the business.

One thing I can promise you is that skills cannot be learnt by looking at a PowerPoint screen, or by being involved in group work and discussion.

Skills are learnt by practice

So, if you are going to gain a quick victory, it will be by getting your delegates practiced and reinforcing the learning.

Step 22 ACTION PLAN - DISCOVER THE SECRETS TO QUICK VICTORIES

Identify the areas that will give you the highest value return

STEP 23 – Max the benefits from your budget

- **Box clever!**
- **Relate budget to importance**
- **What if I don't?**

Box clever!

It is proven by the Chartered Institute of Personnel Development (CIPD) that learning retention is increased by 70% when training is followed by coaching.

This is what I mean when I say you need to **box clever**. Your budget needs to be employed to gain you the highest level results from the highest value activities.

The solution? Review your budget as follows:

Where will you gain the highest value return?

- Which topics?

- Which delegate group?

How will you allocate funds to these areas for the best ROI?

In other words, split the budget according to the best value and the quick victories.

Relate budget to importance

It is a simple method, but actually rather obvious. You allocate the budget according to the relative importance.

This may seem scary, but it is precisely the right business thinking. You may end up investing 40% of your allocation for management development to Praise and Reprimand only! However, this will probably allow you to provide:

- A workshop - divided into two - first half would be learning the concepts and the second half practicing.
- Follow up coaching
- A webinar or other follow up
- A short follow up workshop for skills assessment and honing.

Just imagine, if all of your managers were highly competent in praising and reprimanding, what would it mean?

- Your staff would perform better, as they would have clear guidelines.
- Your staff would be happier and morale would be higher   they would take less time off, there would be fewer problems for the HR department, ultimately fewer tribunals or grievances and so forth.

- Your managers would improve in their performance and they would feel more confident and have increased morale.

You can only achieve this if you fully support a process from concept to skills development to practice. And provide on-going support to really embed this learning in the workplace.

What if I don't?

When you begin to look at the benefits this approach appears more obvious. However, when you look at the negative consequences, it becomes really compelling.

If you do not get these skills in place the negative results can be:

- Relations can be strained to the point of breaking.
- Conflict and confrontation
- High costs in handling conflict resolution
- High costs of underperformance of staff
- Time/Cost of managers carrying out ineffective staff management - longer time taken to achieve the same thing if you're lucky, but most likely, less effective results.
- Poor business profile
- Loss of able staff
- Dissatisfaction and low morale
- Time spent in fire fighting

Ask HR, I bet they can tell you about the time and cost of these outcomes!

Step 23 ACTION PLAN - ALLOCATE YOUR BUDGET FOR MAXIMUM BENEFITS

Proportion your budget according to high value ROI

Chapter 9: The Big Win-Win

Steps 24, 25 and 26

Now we're going to look at how you push on through for the big win-win. This means creating the right blend of learning methods to ensure your people will get the maximum gain. You need to really engage them so that learning – and behaviour change - becomes something they desire, and seek out. You need to share! Look at ways of diffusing your own love of learning, so it becomes part of your organisation's culture.

Your creativity really comes into play in these three Steps. You yourself need to be a blend of things: resourceful, inventive and practical, ingenious and innovative.

STEP 24 – A Winning Formula

- **Being a pioneer of blending**
- **The golden rule!**

Being a pioneer of blending

I have been involved in blended learning for 20 years, and it is no exaggeration to say that I am a pioneer, having been quoted in Prime Minister Tony Blair's Our Information Age booklet as an example of excellence. I was developing e-learning packages as part of government schemes nearly 20 years ago.

Having said all that, I would like to make it very clear that I do not think that e-learning is any replacement for classroom learning and coaching. After 20 years I have come to the very clear conclusion that if you want to develop skills then you can only do this with practice, practice, practice! And that is NOT something that can be achieved in front of a computer - not, at least, if you're trying to develop management and communication skills.

The secret to using blended learning is:

- To ensure that you focus maximum attention on the areas that give maximum pay off
- That you identify the areas that benefit from different forms of training.

The golden rule!
Focus on skills in the classroom, attitudes in coaching and knowledge in other forms such as webinars and other e-learning tools.

When you are structuring your programme you need to be considering the approach learners may be making to the session.

How do you structure your programme for maximum engagement?

- Engage them before the workshop/classroom learning begins.
- Maximise investment by providing intense knowledge inputs via vibrant e-learning tools—such as well produced webinars or using Skype.
- Provide intense practical skills learning and practice in the classroom.
- Follow up learning with consolidation/action plan/implementation coaching.

Note down the main elements of your programme taking these issues into account.

Step 24 ACTION PLAN – A WINNING FORMULA

Make sure you select the right blend of learning to fit your programme

STEP 25 – Be resourceful: use them right!

Do half as much, right

1. Engage the delegates FIRST

2. Knowledge inputs

3. Practical workshop

    o   How to avoid pandering to insecurities

    o   Mistakes are praised

    o   Top tips for creating a learning atmosphere

    o   Close that knowing-doing gap

    o   Physician, heal thyself…

4. Coaching

    o   What does it involve?

Do half as much, right

You have to determine what resources you need to use for each aspect of the programme.

Without a doubt people are the most expensive resource, so make sure you use them where you can get the best return on your investment.

Use on-line and other resources where they will create the best high value results, and most importantly, remember you cannot get a lot for a little. Do half as much training and do it right. This is a far better investment that a full schedule that is not quite all it could be.

1. Engage the delegates first

You would benefit from structuring a programme so that you begin by engaging their interest. I do this by supplying an e-assessment tool. This provides a self-assessment in a topic or attitude relevant to the course. How does this succeed in gaining engagement?

We are all infinitely interested in ourselves. And so a fun tool that gives you an insight into yourself is bound to be a winner.

By using one of my e-tools (which I call Psimplometric™) I manage to get people to engage in the course before they attend. They only take a few moments to complete—so this is also encouraging for busy delegates who are already bogged down with work; they are interesting and fun; and they usually arrive at the course clinging a print out of their results excited about what we are going to do next with them.

2. Knowledge inputs

Few organisations know how to use e-learning most effectively. Some are very committed to e-learning, almost to the exclusion of all else. Others do not really understand it and so avoid it.

The clever way to use e-learning ensures you make the best of its benefits and avoid the drawbacks. This means you have to reconsider the way in which you structure your training.

You may currently run courses that involve a varied mix of input, discussion, practice. This also leads to e-learning being a similar mix (or attempt at this) which will never work.

E-learning can give people quick-fire information, but you cannot make changes to attitude or behaviour with that alone. And you cannot make changes to attitude and behaviour through a computer- well not very easily.

If you are going to get the best from your investment in learning you may have to re-vamp your courses. For example, you can focus all the key learning points into the webinar or teleseminar, and focus the entire workshop on role play and practice.

3. Practical Workshop

I cannot stress strongly enough the importance of practice.

The last thing you want is a group of motivated delegates who leave your training and became disillusioned by their inability to use their learning effectively. And that is something I know my clients have said they have previously experienced. They tell me about training sessions they have run that were brilliant, that the delegates loved them, that they included loads of really "good learning" but when I ask did it make a difference they become circumspect and say "it's difficult to say". To me, that means "No".

The fact is, delegates do not find it very comfortable to practice skills, and for this simple reason: they will get it wrong!

Naturally, the more insecure the delegate feels the more worried they will be about getting it wrong and the less they would want to participate in role plays and other forms of practice.

How to avoid pandering to insecurities

At this point we need to just take a deep breath and ask ourselves "what are we doing in this job?" If the answer is people development, then you HAVE to find a way to get over this problem—and I don't mean by avoiding it and pandering to the delegates preferences.

How will they ever improve if they don't try new things and practice them until they get it right? Would we let a doctor perform if we were not convinced they had practiced "in the classroom" and then with supervision before letting them loose on a patient? Would you present a theoretical paper to a brick layer and then let him or her loose on a building site?

Obviously, the answer is no. And this should be no different in your organisation. By allowing managers who have not practiced and fully developed skills loose on your staff you are risking your businesses reputation, your loyal staff and even your money if you end up in court! You also risk the cost of the time that is wasted in repairing unnecessary damage to relationships. And so on.

Mistakes are praised

My best advice is to make it clear to people that practice is essential, and that errors and mistakes are to be made in the classroom; that the reason for practicing in the class is so that they can try NEW things in a safe environment.

You must foster a learning room atmosphere in which errors or failings are seen as fantastic learning experiences; and that people who are brave enough to try something new, are acknowledged for their sterling efforts; even when they get it "wrong" and learn from their mistakes they are praised because they are going through the essential learning process.

I find that you can create the right atmosphere for this kind of learning, even with insecure delegates.

Top tips for creating a learning atmosphere

A. Start with an exercise that consolidates the workshop's ethos - i.e. one in which you seek out the strengths in each delegate.

B. Tell delegates that they are *allowed* to make mistakes - that they are recognised for identifying what and when they may "get things wrong".

C. Allow delegates to start gently - such as by having a discussion around subject of the role play. When I facilitate this kind of session I say to the syndicate group "so what sort of thing would say there, then?" and allow them to "write the script" before they try it. The funny thing is, they often just "go into a role play" naturally, and without realising they are doing it!!

Never make role play a performance - instead allow people to go off and do them quietly.

And soon they will be prepared to share their experiences but only if you...

D. Make it fun! Learning should be fun, and learning is far more effective when people relax and enjoy it. So work hard and laugh a lot.

E. Reward people who are willing to "have a go". Provide endless amounts of encouragement, but also ensure you give balanced feedback. When you are teaching skills you cannot allow people to think they are performing when they are not. Remember, you wouldn't want a doctor to be told "you're doing a brilliant job!" when he has just administered a fatal dose!

F. Give plenty of time to practicing. This is the most important thing that your delegates will do. It will move them from just knowing to doing.

Close that knowing-doing gap

Practicing skills shifts people across that "knowing-doing" gap which is so prevalent in organisations today. And the reason it is such a vast gap is because time is not given to embedding skills.

The most important thing you can do is give time and keep people on task, ensure they evaluate in a meaningful way, and, although you do not want them sitting at the front of the class "performing" you do need to see that they have adopted the skill, and that they understand what they have done and why it would work.

Physician, heal thyself…

After all this, it is vital for me to say that if you are not extremely well skilled yourself in the subject matter it is very difficult to carry out a skills workshop.

Running a course that involves some input and some role play is straightforward for a skilled facilitator; running a skills workshop is an entirely different matter. If you do not know the strategy and skills involved in, for example, delivering an excellent reprimand, one that motivates the individual and makes them think about their behaviour (and not the "reprimander") AND if you are an excellent facilitator, then you are the one to run the workshop. Or, for example, if you are a skilled and experienced speaker then you are the one to teach presentation skills. If not, get in a professional, make sure they can prove they know what they are doing.

Don't waste time on false economies. Remember the John Ruskin quote from chapter 8.

Finally, make sure the delegate completes an action plan, identifying what and how they are going to implement and embed their learning.

4. Coaching

I've already mentioned the value of follow up coaching, but the secret to making this a success is dependent upon how you will dovetail this with all your other interventions. The coaching should be an integral part, and not an 'add on'.

I recommend you ensure that all your delegates sign up to this while on the workshop, so that they know the time and date of their coaching session. I mostly carry these out by telephone, one-to-one, however, you can also do group calls and face to face.

What does it involve?

The coaching should involve reviewing the action plans that the delegate has created in their practice workshop, talking about the overall experience, and providing time for them to consolidate the experience in their own minds.

Often when you ask a delegate about what learning they have implemented from the training, the delegate will say that they have not had the time to implement anything. However, a skilled coach will tease out of a coaching conversation examples of where skills have been used; the coach will help the delegate to evaluate their performance and by acknowledging their progress this the coach helps to increase the delegates sense of their own success, increases confidence and galvanises their commitment to continuation.

I use a very skilled telephone coach for carrying out this part of the intervention, she knows exactly how to build confidence and reveal the delegates own "truths" whilst remaining supportive and encouraging. The coaching sessions are confidential, and the notes that come out of them at the end are agreed by both parties, but areas that the delegate does not want exposed to management are kept on "pink paper" in other words, they are for the eyes of delegate and coach only.

By building confidence in this way we have had tremendous success with our post training coaching. Again, if you do not have the essential coaching skills, find someone who can do this for you, it is an exceptionally good value investment which creates high level returns,

I have spent over 20 years developing blended learning, and so you can use my strategy to save you re-inventing the wheel.

Step 25 ACTION PLAN – BE RESOURCEFUL: USE THEM RIGHT!

Use your budget and resources wisely, reduce the amount and go for quality.

STEP 26 – Making them want it

- **Leading a horse to water**
- **It's not about you, it's about them**

Leading a horse to water

Earlier on I told you why I think you should be offering training and development according to the needs of the business and not the desires of the delegates; however, if you are going to get delegates engaged and attending your courses you have two choices:

1. You make them mandatory
2. You make them compelling.

If you choose 1, it is fairly straightforward, although you will want them to be engaged in the programme – and as the saying goes, you can lead a horse to water, but... So in any event, you will always benefit from making the title of the course interesting.

The big mistake made by learning and development professionals is in offering things to delegates that relate to competencies and learning outcomes that their *managers* may like, but that *they themselves* will not get excited by. And the course titles are a case in point.

There may be people who simply want to attend a course on "Business Writing Skills", but when it comes to Delegation, for example, some people will want to attend that course, but others may think "I already know all about that". Hmm, well they may know all about it, but are they DOING IT?

It's not about you, it's about them

This is where your bundles of creativity come in! You need to use titles that motivate. Some ideas for developing course titles may be:

- Make a big promise: "Sell 100% more in a week"
- Offer to reveal secrets to the attendees: "The Secrets to Successful Negotiations"
- Be intriguing: "What no one ever tells you about gaining promotion"

When you have your title then you need to offer the learning outcomes in a way that will appeal to your audience, NOT in a way that appeals to YOU!

Yes, it's easy to forget that you are MARKETING to your delegates. So have a good look at the way other people sell their courses, and invest your creativity in designing the perfect title, and in communicating the outcomes so that they are motivating and exciting.

- Tell them that they may currently be making mistakes: "learn the most common mistakes made in communication and how to avoid them."

- Use reverse psychology - tell them NOT to attend if they are not prepared to change: e.g. "This course is not for you if you are not a proactive thinker ready and willing to try new ideas."
- Be specific and use numbers: 5 new ways, 7 mistakes, 3 essential formulae.
- Tell people what they will learn without revealing what it is you will be teaching.

In other words avoid: "How to be effective in Situational Leadership"

Instead try something like: "The four stage magic formula to effective leadership". Or "How to become the leader all your staff will want to follow". Or "Four simple steps to effective leadership". And so on.

Step 26 ACTION PLAN – MAKING THEM WANT IT

Engage your creativity in devising course marketing literature that will SELL!

Chapter 10: Everyone Can Be Saved!
Steps 27 and 28

Nearly there! There are still two more vital Steps, which involve a bit of quiet, followed by a bit of loud.

Reflection is your time for quiet: check out what you've done. We all know that frequently, first goes are just that: a 'go'. There may well be a need for refinement. Now's the time to pick that up, and work on it.

Once the reflection and revision has happened, it's time to get yourself a bit loud and proud. TELL people about what you're doing! It *is* interesting. You've spent time converting what you instinctively know to be true, into a robust, evidence based management development programme that will prove its own worth, time and time again.

And if you don't tell people, who will? Only you can save your job!

STEP 27 – Reflecting on the Process

- **Start with a cuppa**
- **Something is better than nothing**
- **Happy sheet time!**

Start with a cuppa

Reflection is a vital, but much forgotten, part of the overall process. This does seem like a bit of a cop out, I mean, after all that frenetic activity getting your management development programme together, this could almost seem like time for a cuppa!

Well, actually, that is a jolly good idea. You really must take some time out to review where you are at, and this is not as relaxed as it sounds. But start with that cuppa, and look over everything you have done so far.

Does it all fit? Does your programme "feel" right? Does it seem to hold together, look good to you, does it resonate with you?

- Are there gaps that you skipped that will need filling?
- Have you got the buy-in you need from management?

Once you have looked through the entire programme, then you should just write down everything that comes into your mind. Make this a stream of consciousness. You don't need to qualify anything, just note it down, allow your subconscious to work by not *trying* to think. Just relax and muse - oh and have that cuppa!

Something is better than nothing

The next stage is to go through each of your notes and decide if it is:

- An essential change or adjustment
- Requiring input from another party
- An area where you can increase value

Once you have decided how useful your analysis is go back to the plan and make any alterations. BUT do not try to rework it just because you think you have a better idea. NO! This is the fatal error that is made in business. Remember, Microsoft are the biggest supplier of software in the world, but they always release their new products with glitches. They are never 100% perfect. If you wait for perfection, you will have missed the boat, and you may THINK you know what's best, but actually, the best way to find out is by trying it and getting feedback.

So this process is only to ensure that there is a flow and no nasty gaps between which you and your delegates may fall.

Using your subconscious for this stage will allow you to very quickly find those areas that need attention.

Happy sheet time!

Those dreaded things… what you need to do now is devise a feedback form for your delegates, that will actually tell you what you *need* to know.

Cut out unnecessary questions. Remember, this process is intended to help you to improve the delivery so that it better meets business needs, NOT so that it panders to delegates! Harsh, but only fair.

Your delegate action plans should be an important part of the feedback process - in other words, have they completed what they said they would?

I get quite frustrated when I see delegates using a "shoot the messenger" approach. The facts are, (i) delegates need to take responsibility for their learning, and (ii) that they are not the best ones to judge the ability of a trainer. After all, you would not ask someone unqualified to judge your performance, but you may ask them to judge your level of customer service.

I don't expect my solicitor to ask me, "Do you think I have a good knowledge of the law, and do you think I gave you the right advice?" But I would expect to be able to answer if they had treated me respectfully, explained things in an appropriate manner and been supportive and helpful in all their dealings.

Likewise, delegates may not be best qualified to say whether a trainer is competent (but they can often say if they are incompetent - because it stands out a mile).

So do not give the delegates powers that they cannot effectively use. Empower them in terms of what they have *learned* and how they can *use* it.

Yes, ask them if they enjoyed the sessions, if they learnt something new. But I prefer to ask clear questions, because it is too easy to say "no" or "nothing". So how about "what inspired you today?" You usually get some good and interesting answers to that one. "What challenged you?" this may give you answers that are good and bad but that may not be something you need to change—challenging can be good.

Step 27 ACTION PLAN – REFLECTING ON THE PROCESS

- The first step in evaluating your results is in allowing yourself to reflect.
- The second stage is to gain feedback - which will not happen until you are up and running.

STEP 28 – Raising Your Profile

- **Shout it out!**
- **What you are doing is INTERESTING**
- **Why you should start disseminating early result**
- **All publicity is good publicity...**
- **Don't keep it to yourself**
- **The most important thing you can do!**

Shout it out!

This is where you can benefit from your success. It is rare for the Learning and Development team to actively work on raising their profile. This is not because they have not made a difference, had excellent results or made great improvements to the businesses results. No, it's usually because they "don't have time" and another new project is being put across the desk.,

I want you to understand the vital importance of the dissemination of your results; the reasons why you should not wait until you have had proven success, and the benefits to your entire business and most especially the employees.

What you are doing is INTERESTING

It has taken me years to appreciate that what I have to offer is interesting to people, and that people want to hear about my successes. So I come from a rather diffident way of working and thinking.

It was when I got involved in ground breaking work that I realised how vital it is to TALK about what you have done. In talking you involve people in the debate, you gain interest and engagement, and importantly, you gain feedback.

Dissemination is the best form of advertising. The more you talk about what you have achieved, the more interest you gain and the more delegates you will have lining up to attend.

You also gain credibility, just by the process of starting that all important conversation!

Why you should start disseminating early results.

The whole point of dissemination is to build a groundswell of interest, and help people to feel involved.

If you don't have one, get a video camera NOW and interview delegates who attend courses. Interview people's reactions to the programme outlines. ANYTHING that will encourage people to TALK about your work.

If they have negative feedback, get that too, and then disseminate both the feedback and your reaction. You may change things, you may not. The important thing is that you are making a splash!

All publicity is good publicity…

…if it is carefully managed. I have appeared on radio, TV and in national as well as local press, in global newsletters on the Internet, and all because I was disseminating what we were doing - and doing it with PASSION! I have spoken at large conferences for the Department of Trade and Industry, been interviewed on the stage by Kate Bellingham, and appeared on TV running workshops in Uganda.

All these activities have, in their individual ways, created a groundswell of interest. In Uganda I had a disastrous situation where the Chamber of Commerce had let me down and had not arranged any workshops for their members. So I got out my laptop, wrote a press release and got people attending some free workshops. Then I managed to get on national TV running those workshops.

At home, the Department of Trade and Industry were so impressed with my work that they asked me to speak about it, to show case my project as an example of excellence - because I shouted about it from the roof tops. So much so that the UK prime minister's office heard about my project and wanted to know more.

Don't keep it to yourself

This is the secret. You need to talk about what you do. It doesn't have to be perfect, it just needs to be workable. It doesn't need to be big, it just needs to be complete. It doesn't have to be the most original, it just has to be happening!

You can make it happen, and you can make a difference. You have an opportunity to make a real difference to the business and the people within it.

Making a difference doesn't come from being too clever, it comes from applied thinking and ACTION. Making a decision and acting upon it.

The most important thing you can do!

Yes. Making a decision! That is the most important thing you can do. Use your judgment and make a decision, and make sure that decision is TO ACT!

Throughout this book I have referred to Praise and Reprimand as key skills and given them as examples. If you do nothing else, make this an essential skill that you are actually developing the workplace. Not just another one on a list of courses. I say this with good reason.

It is very tempting to try to do EVERYTHING - the fact is, you never can.

You can make the biggest difference to your business, to your managers and to your colleagues by just getting the art of feedback right, and more than anything, the art of giving negative feedback. It is an art, and it therefore has to be practiced and developed.

I urge you to give maximum importance to this key area - even if that is the only thing you do, you will leave a fabulous legacy for your business. Think about the cascading benefits that come from this skill. It is not an easy thing to do, but if everyone knew how to do it right, the effects would be AMAZING!

Please do not become one of

those who start full of great ideas. Remember, this programme is about getting to the end, about producing something - even though you KNOW it will not be perfect, even though you KNOW you will need to adapt and to modify and to keep it alive.

So bear in mind this from one of the most successful business men in the world:

"Nothing in the world can take the place of persistence.

Talent will not; nothing is more common than unsuccessful individuals with talent.

Genius will not: unrewarded genius is almost a proverb.

Education will not: the world is full of educated derelicts.

Persistence and determination alone are omnipotent.

Without persistence life is merely housekeeping."

Ray Kroc

And finally remember that the key to winning is BEGINNING!!!!

Step 28 ACTION PLAN – RAISING YOUR PROFILE

- Get your message out there immediately, and get people talking about the programme.
- Believe in the Power of People Skills and get started on your journey.
- Save your job **NOW** because without you, how can you save everyone else's?

Maria Paviour's CARI™

Commitment and Resilience Index ™
- Gives insights into the barriers to emotional engagement at work
- Identifies where people may be suffering from psychological wellbeing issues.
- Provides the solutions to both

If you want to find out more just call me and I will answer all your questions on: +44(0)1825 830884. Or visit my website, www.mariapaviour.com

Keep in touch!

W mariapaviour.com
T @MariaPaviour
LI MariaPaviour
B mariapaviour.wordpress.com